THE AGA SEAFOOD COOKBOOK

FOR ISOBEL

THE AGA SEAFOOD COOKBOOK

MITCHELL TONKS

PHOTOGRAPHY BY JASON LOWE

ABSOLUTE PRESS

First published in Great Britain in 2005 by
Absolute Press
Scarborough House
29 James Street West
Bath BA1 2BT
Phone 44 (0) 1225 316013
Fax 44 (0) 1225 445836
E-mail info@absolutepress.co.uk
Website www.absolutepress.co.uk

Publisher Jon Croft
Commissioning Editor Meg Avent
Designer Matt Inwood
Publishing Assistant Meg Devenish

Photography Jason Lowe

A catalogue record of this book is available from
the British Library

ISBN 1 904573 25 8

Printed and bound by Butler and Tanner, Frome,
Somerset

CONTENTS

INTRODUCTION

Thankfully, after many years in the doldrums, cooking and eating seafood is the subject of much interest and debate in Britain today. For too long, seafood has been perceived to be inaccessible and somehow difficult to cook. This is a mistake and has blighted our enjoyment of one of the great gastronomic experiences. Eating fish is about delicate flavours, texture and provenance. It is about freshness and clean, simple flavours. It is about avoiding overpowering and dominant flavours and letting the fish do the talking.

A mistreated piece of fish on any cooker is a disappointment. But cooked properly at the right heat, so that the outside crisps and roasts whilst the flesh within is moist and succulent, is a truly great treat. However, it doesn't matter what cooker you've got, unless you start with the best of ingredients, the results will all be the same. Disappointing! So the golden rule is, find a source of really good fresh fish. This will prove to be the most invaluable investment of your time.

Until recently I had always cooked on a gas range. But when I first looked over an Aga, I found that I couldn't wait to cook on one. I could immediately see the extra possibilities it could bring to cooking seafood. The Aga is a perfect tool for fish and shellfish and is ideal for both the cook with a busy life and one with time to spare. Cooking seafood on the Aga is easy. I love to just throw spankingly fresh pieces of fish and shellfish straight on top on the simmering plate along with some herbs, some olive oil and sea salt. The results are brilliant.

Go to any tapas bar in Spain and that plate of wonderfully golden squid, brushed with oil and parsley, and those prawns, coated with salt and olive oil with that wonderful rich shellfish flavour – they will have been cooked on a 'plancha', which is no more than a simple, flat grill.
The nearest thing we have to it in the domestic kitchen is a dry frying pan, but somehow it is just not the same. Lift the simmering plate lid on your Aga, however, and lay some Bake-O-Glide on the top and you will have created the perfect seafood plancha. A plancha that gives you so much flexibility, which will cook fish in such a way that little oil is needed and will result in a wonderful crispy, golden finish.

In the roasting and simmering ovens of the Aga, heat is radiated from all of the sides and in particular the bottom where you can fry and roast, or poach and roast at the same time. I have made great fish soups in the simmering oven and fish pies get a wonderful glazing by being baked properly; while side dishes, such as fennel baked in cream, always come out making you want to dig into them immediately.

I took a lot of persuading that the Aga was right for me.
Things hadn't been helped by my very first experience of cooking fish on an Aga. I was in a theatre in London quite a few years ago, where I was giving a fish cookery demonstration to about 250 people. I arrived on stage where I knew a gas hob and an Aga were waiting. I had planned to cook a roasted fish dish in the Aga and a wonderful Spanish fish stew, called a Zarzuela, on the gas hob. I prepared my fish for roasting, put it into the bottom oven of the Aga (which I embarrassingly know now to be the simmering oven not the roasting!) and went back to the hob to get on with my showpiece stew, informing the audience that the Aga was not the tool for cooking seafood. (How wrong was I?) When I removed the fish, hardly surprisingly, it wasn't cooked and so I again got involved in a bit of Aga bashing, making the point that Agas were best suited to heating farmhouses and baking cakes. This disastrous experience, borne out of ignorance, in front of so many people, put me off Agas for years.

If you have felt that fish is difficult to cook, take my word for it, it isn't. Handle it confidently, and don't worry about it spoiling quickly, it is quite forgiving. Once you have understood the basics, the same rules apply to cooking almost any fish. And as you eat and cook more, and start to understand the individual textures and flavours of each species, you will soon find that you will be able to create easy and simple recipes of your own, from whatever ingredients you have to hand, with increasing confidence and success.

I hope this book will inspire you to cook more seafood on your Aga and make the best out of the fabulous fish and shellfish caught around our shores, which I passionately believe to be the best in the world.

Mitchell Tonks
June 2005

A FISH COOK'S LOOK AT THE AGA

The Aga is really versatile when it comes to cooking seafood. I really love just being able to open the lids, throw bits of seafood on the top and cook them to perfection in just a few minutes. I like to be able to cook stews in the simmering oven, and I love the moistness of a tail of roasted monkfish. It's great that a rich shellfish and tomato stew does no harm slowly simmering in the bottom oven, gently bringing out the wonderful rich flavours from the shells of the crustacea. When you approach cooking seafood, look at the Aga like this:

THE TWO GREAT STARS OF THE AGA

The simmering plate – the 'plancha'
This is a fine way to cook seafood. Lobsters, prawns and langoustines split in half cook best, shell side down. Allow the meat to almost poach in the shells, thus retaining loads of flavour – the heat gives a wonderful caramelisation as they are turned over at the last minute to finish cooking. Whole Dover sole, fillets of hake, and just about any other fish really benefit from this quick kind of grill/frying. Mussels tossed in olive oil and salt and thrown straight on the plates quickly pop open and are wonderful eaten from the shell, dipped in aioli or mayonnaise. The beauty of the Aga is that it is so easy to cook like this – just cut a piece of Bake-O-Glide, big enough to go over the simmering plate (the purpose-cut circular pieces are fine). Never put oil directly on top, instead rub the fish with olive oil, salt and any flavourings and put it straight onto the Bake-O-Glide. If the fish is particularly thick, then colour it first on top, then put it into a roasting tray with a little oil and finish it in the roasting oven. You will need to do this with dense fillets like gurnard and monkfish, and with chunks of brill and turbot. Cod and haddock fillets need colouring only once on one side, but are also best finished off in the roasting oven because of the soft delicate nature of their flesh.

The roasting oven

I know it has always been called this, but I want to emphasise just how good the heat in this oven is for roasting fish. I often use the grill pan in the oven, as I find you can get a really crisp skin on the bottom of the fish by doing it this way. First of all, leave the pan on top of the stove until really hot, rub the fish with olive oil and sea salt, pop it in the roasting pan, then place it directly on the bottom of the oven. This ensures that grilling continues while the remainder of the oven roasts and cooks the fish to perfection.

For poaching, just take an oval dish, add some wine and some aromatics, bring to the boil on top of the stove, cover, then put directly on the bottom of the roasting oven. The fish continues to steam and poach with the benefit of all round heat, ensuring perfect cooking.

MY APPROACH TO COOKING AND EATING

I don't get to cook at the FishWorks restaurants like I used to when I first started out. Nowadays, most of my cooking is done at home. Though I am often referred to as a chef, in reality, as I have never had any formal training, I prefer to think of myself as a cook. The food I make is outside of the pressures and restrictions of a professional environment. There are fewer rules in the domestic kitchen and more room for flexibility, creativity and fun. Cooking has been a source of enjoyment to me all through my life and I have always felt it important to do it in such a way that the enjoyment is continued and doesn't become simply relegated to just another chore in everyday life. I am lucky that my wife, Pen, is a great cook. But at weekends the Aga is mine! I am, what you might call, a typical Saturday cook. The whole family heads off to the local farmer's market in Bath, stock up, have a couple of drinks with friends, and then return to a weekend of cooking, eating and socialising. And with five kids to feed, there are rarely quiet meals in our house!

Making it easy is also part of the skill. I much prefer to get all my preparation done early, which allows me to cook in a relaxed way and serve food from the middle of the table. Whole fish, dishes of pasta, bowls of soup and salads all suit this way of eating. I love it when everyone is sitting round expectantly, with warm empty plates, piles of bread and maybe a bowl of taramasalata in front of them, and then for me to simply plonk down a pile of roasted shellfish on the table for everyone to dig into.

You won't find fish stock or any other time-consuming or awkward preparations for any of the recipes in this book. My food is about absolute freshness, seasonality, simplicity and above all flavour and enjoyment, both in the cooking and the eating. I have always said that my recipes should be seen as a set of guidelines, not rules – be flexible and let your own tastes and preferences influence and guide you, because that in the end is what counts.

RED GILLS.
AVOID BROWN ONES.

BRIGHT VIBRANT COLOURS.

CARLA MAY

6.6 Kg

A FEW THINGS TO LOOK FOR
WHEN BUYING FISH

FRESH FISH LOOKS LIKE IT
HAS JUST COME FROM THE
SEA – WET & GLISTENING.

BRIGHT EYES.

FRESH FISH SMELLS
OF THE SEA.

ACCOMPANIMENTS

TOMATO SAUCE FOR FISH

It is really worth making this wonderful tomato sauce in bulk. Make a day of it. Ask your greengrocer for a really nice ripe box of tomatoes. I usually try and avoid Dutch grown varieties as I find they tend to be watery and lacking in flavour. My favourite varieties are Camone or ripe San Marzano. Making tomato sauce is easy and with a few herbs you have a great base for a whole variety of dishes, many of which feature in this book. If you want to make less sauce just halve everything.

Add some good quality olive oil to a large pan. Add four sticks of celery, a finely chopped bulb of fennel, a teaspoon of crushed fennel seeds, 1 finely chopped large onion and 3 cloves of finely sliced garlic. Cook for 5-6 minutes until softened. The secret is not to let it fry – I usually start it off on the boiling plate and then move it to the simmering plate. Add 1 glass of white wine and allow it to bubble and burn off some of the alcohol. Now add roughly chopped tomatoes – 3 kilogrammes of them – a good pinch of dried oregano and a tied bundle of bay, thyme and parsley. Add a little salt, stir together and transfer to the simmering oven to gently simmer for about an hour

After an hour the tomatoes will have melted into the oil. Remove from the heat and pass the sauce through a mouli or through a conical strainer using a ladle. The consistency should be about that of double cream: if it is too thin, put it back in a pan and onto the heat and boil to reduce a little. I preserve the sauce by putting it into sterilised kilner jars, sealing them and then boiling the jars in water for 15-20 minutes. They will keep for about 2 months when preserved in this way.

ROASTED TOMATOES

These roasted tomatoes are wonderful, perfect with simply grilled fish, and well worth making in quantity. The tomatoes are fabulous fried for breakfast or squeezed in pasta – they also make a delicious accompaniment when smothered in Basil and Lemon Pesto (see below). Cut the tomatoes in half, sprinkle them with chopped tarragon, some salt, black pepper and a little olive oil and put them in the simmering oven overnight. Serve at room temperature.

BASIL AND LEMON PESTO

To make the pesto, toast a small handful of almonds and pine nuts in a dry pan. Crush a garlic clove in a pestle and mortar, then add the toasted nuts and roughly crush. Add a small handful of basil, some salt and the zest of a lemon and combine. Drizzle in some olive oil until you have a thick sauce, then add a tablespoon of grated Parmesan. Season with salt and pepper – if you fancy it squeeze some lemon juice in to make the sauce a little more tart. A crumbled dried chilli gives the pesto an added kick.

BUTTER BEANS WITH BASIL AND LEMON

Simply drain a tin of best quality butter beans and mix in a tablespoon of olive oil, a teaspoon of red wine vinegar, a handful of finely chopped basil, the zest of a lemon, 2 tablespoons of crème fraiche and some salt and black pepper. Stir together, being careful not to break the beans, to create a really easy and delicious side dish.

COURGETTES WITH MINT AND CUMIN

Take a couple of courgettes, yellow or green, or a bit of each. Chop into rough chunks, fry in a little olive oil with a teaspoon of dried mint and a teaspoon of ground cumin. Cook gently for 3-4 minutes, take off the heat, put on the lid and allow to soften and steam until soft and tender. Finish with some fresh chopped mint, plenty of salt and a squeeze of lemon juice. This is a great dish that goes particularly well with tuna and swordfish.

LIGHTLY PICKLED CUCUMBER WITH DILL

Slice the cucumber thinly. Take 3-4 tablespoons of white wine vinegar, add a tablespoon of sugar and dissolve it. Mix this with the cucumber and leave for 30 minutes. Add a pinch of salt and a small handful of finely chopped dill. Fennel fronds and celery leaves also work well pickled in this way.

GREEK SALAD

I find a Greek salad to be a good accompaniment with just about any simply cooked fish, most especially red mullet. Take a good fresh round lettuce, some cucumber, sliced or chopped in chunks (I prefer chunks), some ripe tomatoes, cut into quarters, a handful of good quality black olives (not the tinned variety), some mild red onions, finely sliced, and some good quality Feta cheese. Make a sharp dressing with red wine vinegar mixed 2-1 with good quality olive oil. Toss the salad in this, and sprinkle liberally with dried Greek oregano or thyme.

FENNEL DAUPHINOISE

This is great with just about anything or simply on its own. Thinly slice up a couple of bulbs of fennel, grind a teaspoon of fennel seeds and slice one small onion. Layer these in a buttered roasting dish, pour over some double cream until covered, sprinkle with Parmesan cheese and grindings of black pepper and place in the roasting oven for 20 minutes, then transfer to the simmering oven for an 45-60 minutes.

SLICED FENNEL, LEMON, CHILLI AND MINT SALAD

It is best to use a mandolin for this, alternatively slice the fennel by hand as thinly as you can. Take a bulb of fennel, pull off the tough outer leaves, trim the tops keeping the feathery fronds. With a small knife dig out the core on the bottom, cut the bulb in half and slice the fennel finely. Make a dressing from the juice of a lemon, a small handful of chopped coriander and chopped mint, as much chilli as you like, a pinch of salt and a few tablespoons of olive oil. Pour the dressing over the fennel and leave to macerate in the fridge for an hour. Put the fronds on top and serve.

WHITE BEANS WITH GARLIC

I love white beans and pulses. Their soft texture makes a great combination with fish. Put about 250ml olive oil into a frying pan, add 4 cloves of garlic that have been finely sliced and 1 dried chilli. On the edge of the simmering plate, allow to warm gently until the garlic is starting to turn golden. Add a well-drained tin of beans, a pinch of salt and cook for a further 2-3 minutes until the garlic is crisp, chewy and golden – the beans will have taken on the wonderful flavour of the garlicky oil. Simply finish by adding a small handful of chopped parsley or chives.

GOOSEBERRY VINEGAR

For the gooseberry vinegar you will need 1 litre of good quality cider vinegar, 1kg ripe gooseberries, a good handful of fresh sorrel or baby spinach leaves and the grated zest of 1 lemon. Boil the vinegar for 3-4 minutes and set aside to cool. Wash the gooseberries and sorrel or spinach and pulse to a chunky paste in a food processor. Stir in the lemon zest and just a pinch of salt and then put into a clean jar, large enough to take the vinegar as well. Pour the vinegar over, cover the jar and leave to mature for 3-4 weeks, giving it a shake every now and then. Stain through fine muslin and pour into sterilized bottles with tops that can be sealed. Any sediment that may still be in the vinegar will settle in a few days.

FISH RECIPES

FISH COOKED IN SALT

Fish cooked in salt is a must for the Aga – it works brilliantly. The salt creates an oven within an oven and the fish cooks by steaming in its own juices. Probably the biggest single challenge is getting enough salt. Coarse rock salt is best and your local pub or restaurant should have a supplier who can get it for you at a reasonable price; or if you are lucky enough to have a local Spanish or Portuguese delicatessen they should be able to supply you. You will need about 2kg of salt for this dish. Fish that work best in salt are sea bass, grey mullet, sea bream (red or black); other fish work well but these are my favourites. It is best to avoid fish with a thin skin as often the salt can penetrate this, adding an unwelcome saltiness. And certainly don't do as I did the first time I experimented, by using fillets! Take a half-size roasting tray and put a layer of salt about 12.5mm thick on the bottom. Then take a fish weighing 450-600g (this is a good portion for one or for 2 to share as a light lunch with salad), that has simply been gutted with scales left on, dry it, then lay it on the salt (stuff the belly cavity with some thyme or rosemary to add flavour). Cover the fish with the remaining salt, sprinkle over some water and place in the top of the roasting oven for 25 minutes. When removed from the oven the salt will have formed a firm crust. Break it with the back of a spoon, it should come off in large chunks revealing the fish. When the fish is exposed, brush the salt away from it with a pastry brush, lift onto a plate and then peel back the skin. Serve beautifully unadorned.

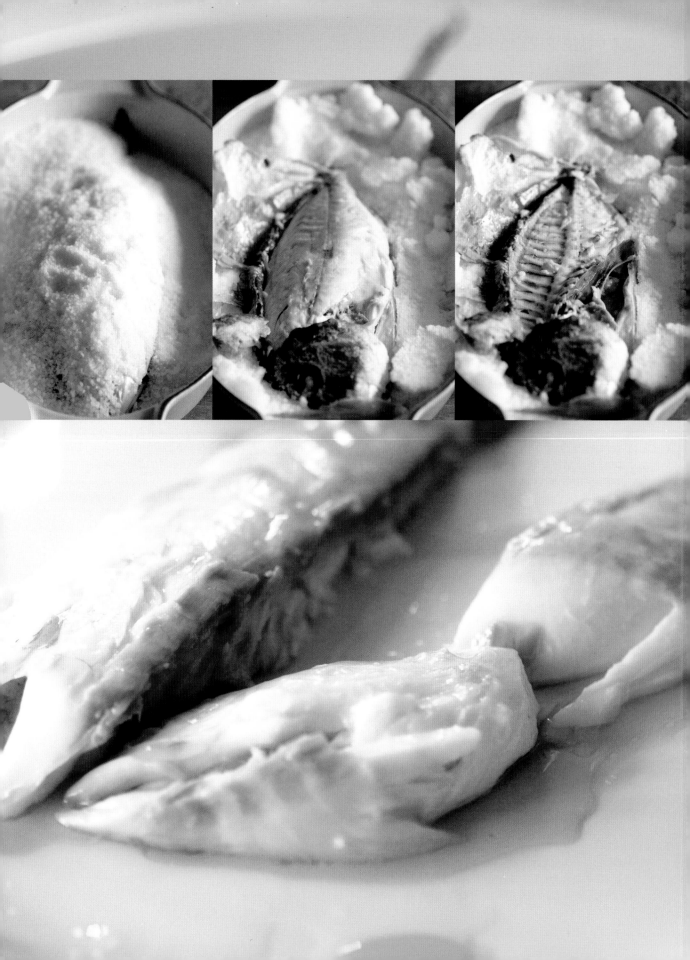

BAKED FISH PIE WITH FENNEL AND POTATO

There are plenty of fish pie recipes, from the very traditional with boiled eggs and smoked and fresh fish in a thick white sauce, to the more 'gourmet' versions, which too often tend to overdo the use of expensive ingredients at the expense of good, honest comfort flavours and texture. For me a fish pie is all about digging into a deep dish of creamy fish and potatoes. Fennel is a great vegetable with fish, which tends to sweeten when cooked, and I have included it in this recipe.

1 leek, chopped
Splash of white wine
1 onion, half of it sliced
4-5 black peppercorns
1 carrot, chopped
2 sticks of celery, chopped
2 fennel bulbs, sliced finely, keeping the root and the top trimmings
1 tsp fennel seeds
Olive oil
25g butter
Some flour
Black pepper
A splash of anchovy sauce (optional)
200g salmon fillet, cut into cubes
200g cod, haddock, whiting or gurnard fillet, skinned and cut into cubes
8-12 mussels, cleaned but in their shells
150g small peeled raw prawns – use cooked ones if these aren't available
Enough mashed potato to cover your dish with about 25cm of topping
Small handful of parsley, finely chopped

First make a vegetable stock by putting the leek, the wine, half an onion, the peppercorns, the carrot and the celery in a pan. Cover with about 500-600ml water and bring to the boil and place in the top of the simmering oven to cook for about 20 minutes. Allow to cool.

While the stock is being made, gently soften the fennel, the sliced onion and the fennel seeds in olive oil in a pan on the simmering plate, until caramelised – you may add a splash of wine or water to help the cooking if needed, but be sure to allow it to evaporate. Cook the vegetables until they are really soft and golden.

Once the stock is ready, place a pan on the simmering plate, melt the butter and add the flour to make a smooth paste, the consistency of double cream. Pour on the simmered stock gently, constantly stirring until you have quite a thick sauce. Season with black pepper and finally add a splash of anchovy sauce, if you are using it.

Butter the bottom of your pie dish and put the fish in, including the uncooked mussels (they will open during cooking, releasing their juices into the sauce). Pour over the sauce, leaving enough room for the potato and fennel topping. Mix the fennel and its juices with the mashed potato, spread on top of the pie and brush with a little butter. Season with black pepper – you could sprinkle over a little Parmesan if liked. Bake for 15-20 minutes on a grid shelf on the floor of the rosting oven. Transfer to the floor of the simmering oven to cook for 20-30 minutes.

Serves 4

ANCHOVY TOAST WITH FRIED DUCK EGG

Anchovy butter is so versatile. Once made and stored in the freezer, it can be melted and finished with a handful of parsley and a squeeze of lemon juice – it is an instant sauce for just about any fish. This is one of my favourite suppers or lunches. Make some anchovy butter in a pestle and mortar by crushing 4 fillets of anchovies, half a clove of garlic and 2-3 rosemary leaves. Make sure you have a pulp (the addition of salt will help break it down but go easy as you have anchovies!). Add this mixture to 50g of soft butter and add a dash or two of Worcestershire sauce. Cut a nice big wedge of white or brown bread, whichever you prefer, and toast it well. Spread with the soft anchovy butter, so that it melts into the toast, then top with a lightly fried duck egg.

BRAISED SEA BASS WITH HOT NORTH AFRICAN SPICES

Whole fish, and it doesn't have to be sea bass, cooked in fiery Moroccan spices are really fabulous. To make this sauce you first have to make this version of harissa, which is delicious and a little different from other versions I have used. Once made, it keeps extremely well stored in a kilner jar in the fridge, with a layer of oil over the top – it can be used when stewing vegetables such as aubergines and peppers to give a bit of a kick, and rubbed into other fish before roasting.

For the harissa
500g tomatoes, cut in half
1 tsp thyme
1 tsp salt
1 tsp cumin
1 tsp ground white pepper
150ml olive oil
500g red peppers
100g dried habenero or jalapeno chillies, or other hot chillies (but not birds' eye)
6 large garlic cloves, peeled
Few tsp tomato purée

1 small onion, finely sliced
2 garlic cloves, finely chopped
1 green pepper, roasted, peeled and cut into strips
$1/2$ tsp of sweet paprika
1 heaped tsp of cumin
Sea salt
2 tbsp tomato purée
1 preserved lemon, cut into chunks
A small handful of parsley, finely chopped
A small handful of coriander, finely chopped
2 sea bass, weighing about 450g each, scaled and cleaned
Olive oil
Lemon juice and coriander, to serve

First make the harissa by roasting the tomatoes with the thyme, salt, cumin, white pepper and olive oil midway in the roasting oven for about 20 minutes. Make some holes in the peppers by stabbing them with a wooden spoon handle. Steam them with the dried chillies and garlic for about 30 minutes until soft. Allow the peppers to cool before peeling them. Put the tray of roasted tomatoes and spices and the steamed pepper, garlic and chillies through a mouli or sieve. Or you could just place it all in a food processor, blitz and then push through a conical strainer. Place this liquid in a pan with a few teaspoons of tomato purée and simmer for a further 5 minutes. It is now ready to use or bottle.

Gently sweat the onions with the garlic until softened. Add the chopped roasted pepper, the paprika, the cumin and the salt. Add the tomato purée and a small glass of water and the preserved lemons and simmer for a further 4-5 minutes. Then add the herbs and 2-3 tablespoons of the harissa – you may add more or less to your taste, though I guess a lot will depend on the heat of the chillies you used!

Place the fish in a roasting tray or, if you prefer, a paella dish (I like using a paella dish as the head and tail curls up at the edges slightly). Pour the contents of the saucepan over the fish and bake in the middle of the roasting oven for about 25 minutes. Serve with a sprinkling of coriander and lemon juice.

Serves 2

SEA BASS WITH ROSEMARY AND CAPER VINAIGRETTE

Rosemary works perfectly with sea bass. Take a sprig or two, remove the leaves and very finely chop them. Put into a bowl with a splash of vinegar and a pinch of sugar. Place in the fridge for a few hours or even overnight. Remove, add a teaspoon of Dijon mustard and gently whisk in some olive oil and add a handful of capers. Take a small bass fillet, rub it with olive oil and put a piece of Bake-O-Glide on the simmering plate. Place it skin side down and cook for 4-5 minutes until golden, turn it and finish cooking for 2-3 minutes. Finally add a squeeze of lemon and serve with a green salad and loads of the vinaigrette.

BAKED SEA BASS WITH ROASTED WHOLE GARLIC, ROSEMARY AND CHILLI

This is a really flexible way of cooking and eating fish, simply baked in a bag. Try this with other types of fish and always include plenty of herbs.

1 sea bass, weighing about 1.25kg, scaled and
   gutted
A few sprigs of rosemary
1 small dried chilli
6 whole cloves of garlic, skin left on
Sea salt
50ml olive oil
$1/2$ a wineglass of dry white wine
1 lemon

Put a piece of turkey-size tinfoil, about 70-80cm long on to a work surface and cover with a layer of parchment paper. Fold over each edge so that the foil and parchment are secured together at the edges.

Put a couple of sprigs of rosemary in the belly cavity of the fish and a couple in the centre of the parchment. Lay the fish on the parchment and crumble the chilli over the top. Lightly crush the garlic cloves by putting the flat side of a knife on top and giving it a thump with your hand, then put them on and around the fish. Sprinkle with sea salt. Lift up the edges of the foil to keep everything in and add the olive oil and wine. Now encase the fish in the foil – it should be in a loose bag but sealed tightly, enabling it to steam. Place it on a roasting tray and bake in the roasting oven for 35 minutes.

Remove from the oven and carefully undo the bag, folding back the sides to make the fish easy to get at. Squeeze a little lemon over the top and give everyone a plate so they can help themselves.

Serves 4

ROASTED SEA BREAM STUFFED WITH SPICES AND SPRING ONIONS

This unusual combination of spices works really well stuffed into the belly of the fish before roasting.

1 tsp ground cinnamon
4-5 black peppercorns
Salt
Small handful of fresh coriander
Small handful of fresh parsley
Handful of fresh breadcrumbs
100g of whole almonds
4 spring onions, finely sliced
1 tbsp ground cumin
2 sea bream, about 450g each, scaled and
    gutted
Olive oil
Lemon juice

Put everything except the fish, olive oil and lemon juice in a food processor and blend until you have a coarse stuffing. Moisten with olive oil and lemon and stuff the mixture in the belly cavity of the fish.

Place the fish in a roasting tray, drizzle with olive oil and place in the middle of the roasting oven for about 20 minutes. Remove and serve with a simple salad.

Serves 2

POACHED WHOLE SEA BREAM WITH SAFFRON AND WHITE BEANS

A gilt head sea bream is one of the prettiest and tastiest fish there is. Around the end of June and during July they start to show around the South Coast of Britain. The larger ones, weighing up to 2kg, are fabulous roasted whole. The smaller ones, weighing only 200-300g, are extremely sweet and fresh tasting and are perfect for simply poaching, creating a dish which is really like a fish soup but with whole fish in it. Small bass, red mullet and even small flat fish can be cooked in this way.

$1/2$ onion, finely chopped
2 cloves garlic, finely sliced
Olive oil
3 ripe tomatoes, skinned and finely chopped
A sprig of fresh thyme
A sprig of fresh oregano
Splash of dry sherry
A glass of white wine
A good pinch of saffron
Whole sea bream, 200-300g, scaled and gutted
$1/2$ tin of cannellinni beans
Small handful of parsley, finely chopped

Cook the onions and garlic in the olive oil until softened. Add the tomatoes and cook for a further minute. Add the thyme and oregano, then the sherry and boil to reduce and get rid of the alcohol. Add the wine and boil off the alcohol in the same way. Add the saffron and stir well.

Place the fish in the pan and add water, enough to come half way up the fish. Add a few pinches of salt. Simmer for 4-5 minutes on the simmering plate. Carefully turn the fish over, add the cannellinni beans and the parsley and cook for another 4-5 minutes. Season and serve straight from the pan.

Serves 2

STEAMED BRILL WITH CHARD AND GARLIC

This recipe comes from Laura Cowan, my assistant, who is a fantastic cook. Halfway through writing this book, and stuck for inspiration, I asked her what fish dishes she particularly likes to cook for her family and this is the recipe that she came up with – so I shamelessly nicked it and put it in the book when she wasn't looking!

170g swiss chard
3 garlic cloves, finely sliced
2 fillets of brill, weighing about 200g each
Zest and juice of a lemon
1 tbsp very finely chopped basil
2 tbsps olive oil
1 tsp tarragon mustard

Put the chard in the basket of a steamer or petal steamer, sprinkle over the garlic, lay the fish on top, sprinkle with salt and steam for 8-10 minutes on the boiling plate.

Make a dressing with the lemon juice, lemon zest, basil, olive oil and mustard by simply whisking them all together. Drizzle over the fish.

Serves 2

CLAMS WITH BACON AND CORIANDER

Allow about 300-400g clams per person for a starter. Surf clams are my favourite – they have a lovely buff coloured shell. The more expensive palourdes, or carpet clams as they are sometimes known, are equally good but due to their fine and delicate flavour I prefer to eat them raw. Put a splash of wine and half a cupful of water, some chunks or lardons of bacon (even nicer than bacon is chopped Serrano ham if you have any) in a pan. Simmer for 2-3 minutes, add the clams and boil them until they open. Discard any that don't. Add some chopped coriander and stir in well. Thicken the broth with just a little cornflour mixed with water. Season with white pepper and serve.

'BECAUSE OF THEIR FINE AND DELICATE FLAVOUR, I LIKE TO EAT PALOURDES CLAMS RAW FROM THE SHELL.'

GRILLED RAZOR CLAMS

Razor clams cook fabulously on the Aga. Put a frying pan on the boiling plate and add some clams – cook until they pop open. Take out the meat and reserve the juices. Put a piece of Bake-O-Glide on the simmering plate and cook the clam meat for a little longer, just until it takes on a slight golden colour. This extra bit of cooking really enhances the sweetness of the flesh. To serve, place the clams back in their shells, add a little red wine vinegar to the reserved juices, a tablespoon of olive oil, some finely chopped tomato and some finely chopped parsley. Spoon this dressing over the clam meat.

TARAMASALATA

I have been making this ever since I opened my first restaurant and fish shop in Bath nearly 10 years ago and it remains one of our all time favourites with customers. I have also made it at countless cookery schools and always get a thrill at the expressions of enjoyment on the faces of the students as they first try a mouthful. It is a simple dish created by just whizzing things up, adding some oil, then adjusting the creaminess with water. The consistency should be just a little heavier than whipped cream. Serve it with some slices of raw vegetables – fennel works really well. If you want to turn this into a centrepiece starter rather than simply a great dip, then just provide a selection of raw vegetables on a plate for your guests to dig in. Once made, the taramasalata will keep in the refrigerator for a week or so.

2 slices of yesterday's bread, crusts removed
1-2 cloves garlic
Juice of 1 lemon
250g smoked cod's roe
300ml vegetable oil
100ml olive oil
$\frac{1}{2}$ a wine glass of cold water
Chopped parsley or coriander and black olives,
   to serve

Put the bread and garlic into a food processor and switch on, adding lemon juice until you have a smooth paste. Then add the cod's roe, including the skin (which contains a lot of the essential flavour, having been in direct contact with the smoke in the kiln). Keep blitzing until the mixture is smooth and creamy.

Add the vegetable oil in a gentle stream until you have a thick buttery consistency. Slowly add the olive oil – you may find it becomes quite stiff and cloying but don't worry – then add the water slowly until you get the right consistency. If you add too much water and the mixture becomes sloppy, simply drizzle in more oil until you get it right.

Sprinkle with chopped parsley or coriander, a few black olives and serve with bread and raw vegetables.

Makes enough to serve 6-8

SALT COD TOMATO SALAD

I love salt cod. Avoid making this dish with the thinner fillets of fish that are dried hard – keep those bits for cooking and stewing – for this recipe use cod fillets taken from the thicker end of the fish. The texture and flavour of salt cod is fantastic and should have just the right amount of saltiness – the salt is partly for flavour but also alters the texture of the fish. The Spanish hold salt cod in high regard and prime loins of cod are considered the best. I like to make my own by taking a nice fillet of cod, covering it with rock salt for 3-4 days (draining off any liquid which is drawn out during that period). I then soak it for 2 days in cold water in the fridge, changing the water at least 3-4 times. The easy way to tell if the fish is ready, is to cut off a piece of the fish and decide for yourself whether it is too salty. You simply then skin and shred the fish, toss it with half a dozen chopped tomatoes, some cooked green beans, a handful of torn basil leaves, some black olives, a splash of red wine vinegar and some good olive oil and lastly a few slices of hard boiled egg. The addition of roasted sweet peppers is also very good.

.

POACHED COD'S ROE WITH BEARNAISE SAUCE

We should eat more roe. Cod's roe is the most widely available. It is delicious smoked but equally delicious simply poached and served with mashed potatoes, peas and béarnaise sauce.

1 large cod roe, weighing about 750g
$\frac{1}{2}$ a fennel bulb, roughly chopped
1 onion, roughly chopped
A carrot, chopped
1 stick of celery, chopped

For the béarnaise sauce
3 tbsps tarragon vinegar
1 shallot, finely chopped
2 egg yolks
200-300g butter, melted
Small handful of tarragon, finely chopped
Squeeze of lemon juice

Take a piece of muslin cloth, large enough to wrap the roes in. Place the roes at one end and roll up, twisting the ends like a Christmas cracker in opposite directions – if you hang onto these (where you would normally pull a cracker) and roll the cod's roe away from you, the sausage will tighten into a cylindrical shape. Fold the ends on top and then loosely tie with string.

Bring a pan of water to the boil on the boiling plate, add the fennel, onion, celery and carrot and after 2-3 minutes' boiling, cover and transfer to the simmering oven for 15 minutes.

To make the sauce, put the tarragon vinegar and the shallots in a plan, reduce until you have about a tablespoon or so of liquid and strain, keeping the liquid. In a bowl, whisk the egg yolks with a tablespoon of water and the strained vinegar. Hold the bowl with a cloth over a boiling pan of water and whisk continuously until the eggs have doubled in size but not scrambled! Pour in the melted butter while whisking. Add the tarragon and the lemon juice. This sauce should be the consistency of thick double cream.

Remove the roe from the poaching liquid, unwrap it, cut it into slices and serve with the béarnaise sauce, some cabbage, peas or mashed potato.

Serves 4

FRESH CRAB WITH LIME AND ASIAN HERBS WRAPPED IN CRISP LETTUCE

The hardest part of this dish is finding good fresh Asian ingredients. If you are lucky enough to have a Thai supermarket near where you live than that is ideal. It is certainly worth seeking one out because the flavours of the Thai basil and herbs are quite special. This is a dish best served in the middle of the table with a mound of lettuce leaves. You simply pick up the crabmeat, wrap it in the lettuce leaves and eat.

Pinch of sugar
Juice of a lime
1 red chilli, seeds removed, finely chopped
Splash of fish sauce
1 tsp very finely chopped ginger
1 tbsp very finely chopped mint
1 tbsp very finely chopped Thai basil
1 small shallot, very finely chopped
250g fresh picked white crabmeat
1 lettuce

Make the dressing by dissolving the sugar in the lime, mix in the remaining ingredients and stir into the crabmeat. Serve in a dish on the table with plenty of lettuce to wrap it all up in and get your family and friends to dig in.

Serves 4 as a starter

CUTTLEFISH COOKED IN ITS OWN INK

If you go to Venice you will find this wonderfully tasty dish on just about every menu. Don't be put off by the idea of cuttlefish ink. The Venetians love for it is a testament to how good it really is. However, if you really can't stand the thought of the ink then just leave it out. You will be left with a deep rich red tomato sauce. We don't eat nearly enough cuttlefish. Once you have tried it, when cooked properly until soft, it is sweeter and I think more enjoyable than the ever present squid.

Olive oil
2 cloves garlic, finely chopped
1 small onion, finely chopped
1kg cuttlefish, cleaned, but with the ink sacs reserved. Get your fishmonger to do this for you, as it can be messy. If the ink has already burst, (or the fishmonger messed up!) then buy a sachet or two of squid ink
Salt and black pepper
1 glass white wine
2 tbsp tomato purée
2 tomatoes, roughly chopped
1 wine glass of water
1 small handful of parsley

Chop the cuttlefish into strips.

Pour a generous glug of olive oil into a casserole dish. Add the garlic and onion and heat on the boiling plate and then transfer to the simmering plate and cook until lightly golden. Add the cuttlefish and fry for a further minute or two. Season with salt, add the wine and reduce by half. Add the tomato purée and the chopped tomatoes, the water, half the parsley and lastly the ink. Stir together to amalgamate, bring to the boil, cover and put in the top of the simmering oven for about 1 hour.

Remove the casserole dish from the oven. The sauce should be thick and jet black and a fork should push easily into the cuttlefish – if it is still firm, cook for a further half hour or so, or if the sauce is not thick enough, gently boil some of the liquid away. This dish looks stunning when served on white plates and just sprinkled with parsley.

Serves 2

SPRING CABBAGE BROTH WITH SMOKED EEL AND BACON

I love smoked eel, served simply with horseradish or particularly, as they do at Fergus Henderson's brilliant St John restaurant in Clerkenwell, with mash and bacon. It is also quite delicious in this dish and is really simple to make. If you don't like the texture or flavour of smoked eel, then I would see nothing wrong with taking a fillet of smoked haddock, skinning it and cutting it into chunks and using it instead.

1 onion
2 sticks of celery, roughly chopped
2 carrots, roughly chopped
$\frac{1}{2}$ leek, roughly chopped
A few peppercorns
A bunch of thyme, parsley and sage tied
    together
2 thick slices of bacon, cut into chunks
150g smoked eel fillet, cut into chunks
A quarter of a small spring cabbage, blanched
    and refreshed in cold water
1 tbsp parsley, finely chopped
Black pepper
A few tbsp of finely grated Parmesan

Put the onion, celery, carrots, leeks, peppercorn and the herbs in a pan. Cover with water, bring to the boil on the boiling plate and place in the top of the simmering oven for 30 minutes. Strain then season.

Add the bacon and the smoked eel and simmer gently for about 5 minutes, then add the cabbage and the parsley. Season with black pepper. Ladle into bowls and finish with a sprinkling of Parmesan.

Serves 4

GURNARD COOKED IN BUTTER WITH LEMON AND PARSLEY

Gurnard is rightly becoming ever more popular (see previous recipe), but don't be fooled into thinking it's a cheap or economical fish. With a large head and pointed tail, you get a very low yield. I think this fish needs a little help as, when cooked, it has small flakes held tightly together with a tendency towards dryness. Gently poaching or cooking slowly and basting in butter is the way to go with gurnard. Simply take 2 gurnard fillets and lightly flour them.

Melt 30g butter in an oval dish on the simmering plate, add the fish and cook for 5-6 minutes. Turn the fish over, then with a spoon baste the fish and cook for a further 2-3 minutes. Squeeze in the juice of $1/2$ a lemon and a handful of parsley. Put straight into the middle of the table with a bowl of green beans and some new potatoes. This is also a great way to cook lemon sole, whiting or plaice fillet.

ARBROATH SMOKIE HASH

Hard to find but still available, an Arbroath Smokie is a small haddock, hot-smoked and left on the bone. As the name implies, the flavour is smoky and comforting. Flaked into crushed potatoes, with lots of chives and a bit of mustard and a nice duck egg placed on top, the Arbroath Smokie makes a wonderfully creamy and delicious hash.

350ml milk
1 Arbroath Smokie
300g small potatoes
1 tsp Dijon mustard
A few tbsps cream sherry
25g butter
A good handful of chives, chopped
2 fried duck eggs (optional)

Put the milk in a roasting dish with the fish, cover with foil and place directly on the bottom of the roasting oven for 12-15 minutes. Remove and allow to cool.

Bring the potatoes to the boil and simmer for 3-4 minutes, drain, cover and transfer to the simmering oven until tender, about 20-30 minutes. Drain, then put back in the pan and allow the moisture to steam off.

Mix the mustard and sherry together. Melt the butter and gradually whisk it with the sherry and mustard as if making a dressing, then add the chives and a few tablespoons of the milk in which the haddock was cooked.

Lightly crush the potatoes. Peel the skin off the fish, pick off the flesh and add to the potatoes. Stir together with the dressing and add plenty of black pepper. Place a fried duck egg on top of each serving.

Serves 2

SMOKED HADDOCK SOUP WITH POACHED EGG

This is one of our truly great British dishes. It is so simple to make and is amazingly comforting and wonderfully luxurious when the yolk is broken and runs through the soup.

750ml full cream milk
450g good quality un-dyed smoked haddock
1 bay leaf
Small handful of chopped parsley leaves
  (reserve the stalks)
50g butter
1 medium onion, finely chopped
200g creamy mashed potato
Salt and plenty of black pepper
4 eggs

Put the milk in a pan on the simmering pate large enough to take the haddock. Add the bay leaf and parsley stalks, simmer for 4 minutes then leave to infuse for a further 5 minutes. When cool enough remove the haddock, reserving the liquid, and break up into flakes, removing any skin and bone.

Melt the butter in another pan on the simmering plate and cook the onions until soft but not browned. Add the strained poaching liquid then stir in enough mashed potato until you have a thickened creamy consistency. Add the parsley and the haddock and simmer for a further 3-4 minutes. Season with plenty of black pepper (and salt if needed) and serve with a sprinkling of chopped parsley and a lighlty poached egg on top.

Serves 4

'GENTLY POACHING OR COOKING SLOWLY AND BASTING IN BUTTER IS THE WAY TO GO WITH GURNARD.'

SMOKED HADDOCK WITH LEEK AND POTATOES

I can't think of anybody that doesn't like smoked haddock. It makes a brilliant breakfast and kept simple with just a little butter, loads of black pepper and a properly poached egg, is hard to beat. As in this recipe, it goes brilliantly with leeks and potatoes and a good dollop of mustard. Here you just use a couple of tablespoons of creamed leeks, stir them into some mashed potato and then whack a dollop of mustard onto the plate – a great combination.

Butter
2 chunks smoked haddock, weighing about
    250g each
1 leek, washed and finely shredded
150ml double cream
Wholegrain mustard
Enough mashed potato for two
Salt and black pepper
1 tsp tarragon, chopped (parsley also works
    well, as do chives)

Rub some butter over the smoked haddock and place in a roasting tin at the top of the roasting oven for 5 minutes.

Put the leeks in a saucepan on the simmering plate with no oil or liquid – leeks are full of water and they will happily cook in their own juices. (When they are softened it is important to drain off all of the water.) Add the cream and just a teaspoon of the mustard and stir this into the mashed potato along with the herbs.

Finally, melt a little butter and pour over the haddock. Serve with the mash and an extra dollop of mustard.

Serves 2

GRILLED HAKE WITH SPINACH, ROASTED GARLIC AND ANCHOVY SAUCE

Hake is more popular in Spain than in the UK. We should really take more notice of it. Its flesh is delicate, soft and delicious.

2 hake steaks, about 25mm thick
A little butter
6 salted anchovy fillets
4 whole garlic cloves, roasted with olive oil in the roasting oven for 8-10 minutes until soft
1 tbsp double cream
1 tsp fresh oregano, very finely chopped
Juice of 1 lemon
250-300g spinach, washed

The texture of hake allows the fish to be cooked perfectly on top of the stove. Rub the fish with oil, lift the lid of the simmering plate and place a rectangle of Bake-O-Glide on the top (a rectangle will make less mess than using the smaller circle size). Cook the fish either side for about 3-4 minutes.

To make the sauce, melt the butter in a pan, add the anchovies and stir them until they melt into the butter. Squeeze the roasted garlic from their skins into the sauce. Add a tablespoon of cream, the oregano and a squeeze of lemon. Wilt the spinach in a dry pan, drain and serve with the fish and the sauce poured over.

Serves 2

ROASTED HAKE WITH WHITE ONION SAUCE

This is my mum's recipe for onion sauce. It's great with fish, especially the soft textured hake, but is also excellent with skate, rock salmon or cod.

2 chunks of hake on the bone, or fillets if you
    prefer, weighing about 250g on the bone,
    175g off
Sea salt
1$\frac{1}{2}$ large onions, very finely sliced
6 cloves
6 peppercorns
2 bay leaves
500ml milk
25g butter
2 tbsp plain flour
1 handful of parsley, finely chopped

Put the hake steaks in a roasting pan, drizzle with a little olive oil, some sea salt and place in the middle of the roasting oven for 12-15 minutes.

Make the sauce by putting the onions, cloves, peppercorns and bay leaves into the milk. Simmer on the simmering plate for 3 minutes, cover and transfer to the simmering oven for 15-20 minutes until tender. The onions should be completely melted.

In a separate pan on the simmering plate, melt the butter and sprinkle on the flour until you have a smooth roux. Remove from the heat and steadily pour on the hot milk, constantly stirring to ensure there are no lumps. Remove the spices and return to the heat. Season, add the parsley and serve with the fish. Cabbage or broccoli would make a good accompaniment.

Serves 2

FRESH HERRINGS IN A MUSTARD AND CAPER SAUCE

Herring are plentiful in spring and early summer and are pure nutritional bliss all packaged into one silvery, gleaming fish. They can be found easily in farmers' markets and fishmongers around the country. Over the years the humble herring has been rather overlooked, regarded as something annoyingly full of bones. I can't deny that they do indeed have a few small bones, however, picking your way through a fat juicy herring is all part of the fun. Unless they are big, serve a couple of fish per person and try and buy those herring that contain soft roes. The hard roes, which come from the female fish, are slightly grainy, while the roes from the male are beautifully soft and creamy, packed with goodness and really easy to cook. To cook the roes, simply dip them in flour, fry them gently in butter and put them on a piece of toast. Then just add some lemon juice and chopped parsley to the juices in the pan and pour over the top of the roes, thus making a nice easy garnish or starter for your main course herring. Because of its oiliness, herring can stand up to sharp flavours, and this mustard sauce is packed full of piquancy. I would serve the herring with a simple parsley salad, consisting of fresh parsley leaves tossed with olive oil and lemon, finely chopped shallots and maybe a few capers. So, the lesson here is that you should not overlook the humble herring, which in fact is really the King of the Sea in disguise.

4 herrings, about 250g each, cleaned and scaled and heads cut off
1 tbsp dill, chopped
1 small onion, finely chopped
1 small handful of capers
4 gherkins, finely chopped
100ml white wine
100ml water
A small handful of parsley
Lemon juice
1 dessertspoon of English mustard

Take a square of tin foil (the size of the width of the roll). Overlay it with a sheet of greaseproof paper and put the herrings in the middle. Mix the rest of the ingredients in a jug. Fold up the sides of the tin foil and pour in the liquid. Seal tightly so that none of the juices escape and then bake in the roasting oven for 10-12 minutes until the herrings are just moist. Serve with a parsley salad (see introduction to recipe) and some boiled new potatoes to soak up those wonderful piquant juices.

Serves 2

DEVILLED SOFT HERRING ROES

I prefer soft to hard herring roes and think they are the best part of the fish. They can be served on toast or simply on their own. Take 3-4 herring roes per person. Mix 3 tbsp of English mustard with a teaspoon of Worcestershire sauce, brush over the roes, season with black pepper and a little salt and then fry for 2-3 minutes. Serve with a sprinkling of paprika. And if you want a little bit of sauce then just add a splash of cream to the pan juices.

CROSTINI OF SMOKED HERRING WITH ONIONS, CAPERS AND WATERCRESS

I wonder how many people turn their nose up at the thought of kippers? Probably about the same amount as those who are already fans. You love them or hate them. The truth is that kippers (technically smoked herring) are delicious but people simply don't like battling with all the bones. And fish for breakfast, whilst very English, hasn't really caught on – though a well-made kedgeree would certainly be top of my list first thing in the morning. This recipe is an updated version of how we might once again learn to love smoked herring. In fact, I bet if you served these to guests and just referred to them as 'smoked herring crostini', they would be amazed at the smoky caramel-like sweetness of the fish, and maybe even discard once and for all the unjust prejudice against the humble but magnificent kipper.

1 fat juicy kipper
1 tbsp of capers
1 small onion, finely chopped
1 tbsp of parsley, finely chopped
1 tbsp of gherkins, finely chopped
1 tsp of horseradish
Black pepper
A handful of watercress
4 slices of ciabatta, lightly toasted
Lemon juice
Sour cream, to serve
Cayenne pepper

Put the kipper in a roasting dish, cover with boiling water and poach for 5-6 minutes. Leave to cool in the water.

Remove the kipper flesh from the bone and mix with the capers, onion, parsley, gherkins and horseradish and season with black pepper.

Arrange some watercress on top of the ciabatta slices and then put a tablespoon of the kipper mixture on top. Add a squeeze of lemon juice, top with a dollop of sour cream, sprinkle with cayenne pepper and serve.

Serves 2 as a light lunch or 4 as a starter

JOHN DORY WITH SALSA VERDE

In the same league as turbot and bass, John Dory is loved for its firm distinctive flavour. The experience comes at a cost though, with a big head and heavy bones, the yield is low, but in my opinion well worth it. Salsa verde is fabulous with all fish as it really captures the essence of freshness. It is unsurpassed when eaten with grilled fish with crispy skin. You can be pretty flexible with the herbs you use but the traditional combination used here is particularly good.

1 John Dory, weighing about 1kg, head removed

For the salsa verde
1 tsp Dijon mustard
Small handful of parsley
1 tbsp fresh mint
Small handful of basil, finely chopped
4 anchovy fillets, finely chopped
A small handful of capers
Good olive oil
Lemon juice

Put the grill pan on the hot plate and leave for 6-7 minutes to be sure it is really hot – serious heat is the key to the success of this dish.

Rub olive oil and salt into the skin of the John Dory and put the fish in the pan. Cook for 5-6 minutes. Turn once the skin is beautifully crisp and then transfer the grill pan directly onto the floor of the roasting oven and continue to cook for 15-20 minutes - it is cooked when a milky liquid runs from the fish.

Put the mustard, herbs, anchovies and capers in a bowl and gradually stir in the olive oil with a fork, pouring in a gentle stream until you have a thick sauce. Finish with a squeeze of lemon juice.

Remove the fish from the oven, put on a plate, squeeze over some lemon juice and dress with the sauce or serve it alongside.

Serves 2

JOHN DORY ROASTED WITH INDIAN FIVE SPICE

I source my spices from a wonderful company called Sambava Spices, who make a fantastic mix of five Bengali spices called panch phora – literally 'five seeds'. It is perfect with seafood when ground very finely and sprinkled over a fillet and then cooked simply in a pan with a little oil on the boiling plate of the Aga. The measures of the ingredients are 3 teaspoons ground mustard seed, 2 teaspoons nigella seed, 2 teaspoons cumin, 1½ teaspoons fenugreek and 1 teaspoon fennel seeds. Simply roast the spices and grind them finely. Sprinkle over the fish before cooking. I have suggested John Dory fillets, as the fish has a good firm texture and the flavour of the flesh seems to marry particularly well with this mix of spices.

'A BAGFUL OF LIVE AND KICKING LANGOUSTINES MAKE FOR A MEMORABLE MEAL. THEY ARE ONE OF THE MOST DELICIOUS AND SWEETEST CREATURES IN THE SEA.'

GRILLED LANGOUSTINES

By grilling, I mean cooking on the Aga simmering or boiling plate. Langoustines are fantastic cooked in this way and a bagful of fresh live and kicking langoustines make for a memorable meal. Buy them as big as you can afford – they are expensive but worth every single penny. I think they are one of the most delicious and sweetest creatures in the sea.

1-2kg langoustines, depending on appetite
150ml olive oil
Pinch of chilli flakes
1 garlic clove, finely chopped
Good pinch of sea salt
Small handful of parsley, finely chopped
Juice of $\frac{1}{2}$ lemon
Freshly milled black pepper

Split the langoustines in half lengthways by inserting a knife in the back of the head (you will see a little cross) and levering it towards the tail. Turn the langoustine round and separate it at the head. In a large bowl, large enough to hold the langoustines, add 100ml of the olive oil, the chilli flakes, half of the garlic and the salt and mix together. Add the langoustines and mix with your hands to make sure they are well coated.

Place some Bake-O-Glide on the simmering plate and with a pair of tongs put the langoustines shell side down and allow to cook for 4-5 minutes. Turn the langoustines over for 1-2 minutes until the flesh just starts to turn golden. Mix together the parsley, olive oil, lemon juice, salt, black pepper and remaining garlic. Remove the langoustines to a plate and brush the flesh with the parsley and garlic dressing.

Serves 2

BOILED LOBSTER WITH NEW POTATOES AND MINT

This recipe is all about simplicity and the combination of outstanding ingredients. If I've got potatoes that are ready to lift from my garden, then I will be certain to ensure that there is a live native lobster not too far away ready to make this great combination work. Just bring a pan of water to the boil, add a handful of salt, add a live lobster (weighing about 750g) to the boiling pan and give it 10-12 minutes. While the lobster is cooking, boil the new potatoes with a good handful of mint in the pan. Drain and toss in butter with a small handful of finely chopped parsley. Split the lobster in half and serve the two together with a ramekin of melted butter.

SWEET AND SOUR CHILLI-BAKED LOBSTER

The Aga is perfect for this dish. The heat which radiates from all around the oven means that the lobster is boiling and roasting all at the same time in the sweet, hot, sticky sauce. It really is fantastic. You can also try it with some mussels and clams. Simply make the sauce first - steam open your mussels and clams, throwing away the liquid, and finish cooking in the roasting oven until they are well coated.

1 live lobster
Vegetable oil
1 onion, chopped
3 cloves garlic, finely sliced
50mm ginger root, finely sliced, skin left on
4 chillies, sliced
200ml white wine vinegar
100g sugar
2 tbsp Thai fish sauce
A bunch of spring onions, cut into chunks
Juice of 2 limes
A good handful of basil leaves (Thai preferably), finely chopped
A handful of fresh coriander, chopped

Half cook the lobster by dropping it in salted boiling water and cooking for 5-6 minutes. Remove to drain and cool. When cool twist off the claws and crack open with a heavy knife. Cut the lobster down the middle and cut the tail into chunks. Cut the head into two. Put all the meat in a colander and allow any moisture to drain. Don't be alarmed by any green or bright red gunge in the body, it is just the roe of the lobster and is perfectly edible and quite delicious.

Place a cast iron roasting dish on the simmering plate and gently fry the onion, garlic, ginger and chillies until slightly golden. Add the white wine vinegar, the sugar and the fish sauce. Taste, it should be hot, sweet and slightly sour – you will know when it is not right, and will need to add either more sugar or vinegar to your taste. Continue to cook for 3-4 minutes until reduced by about a third. Put the lobster chunks into the dish along with the spring onion and toss thoroughly to make sure they are well coated with the sauce. Place directly on the floor of the roasting oven for a further 6-7 minutes until the sticky sauce coats the lobster. You may want to open the door and turn the lobster every 2-3 minutes.

To serve, remove from the oven, squeeze the lime juice over and toss the lobster pieces with the basil and coriander. Be sure to provide finger bowls!

Serves 2

'MONKFISH COOKS PERFECTLY DIRECTLY ON TOP OF THE STOVE, 'A LA PLANCHA'. JUST A SPRINKLING OF A FEW HERBS AND SOME SALT IS ENOUGH.'

GRILLED BABY MONKFISH WITH BROAD BEAN AND ANCHOVY 'PESTO'

Small monkfish weighing a few hundred grams, are sweeter than the larger ones and often a fifth of the price and well worth buying and hounding your fishmonger for. Ask the fishmonger to skin the monkfish for you. This broad bean accompaniment, that I have called 'pesto', is great with all fish. It can also be made with fresh peas, white beans or borlotti beans. To make the pesto, blanch and peel about 500g broad beans. Put a fifth of them in a blender with 2 cloves of garlic and 4 anchovy fillets and pulse to a coarse paste. Loosen with a little olive oil, add to the remainder of the beans and stir in enough grated Parmesan to your taste and a handful of chopped basil. The whole beans should be just dressed in this mixture. Rub a little olive oil and salt into the fish. Put some Bake-O-Glide on the simmering plate and put the monkfish on top. Allow it to cook for 4-5 minutes until it is golden then turn it over. Serve the monkfish with a tablespoon or two of the pesto and a wedge of lemon.

MONKFISH WITH ROSEMARY AND GREEN PEPPERCORN SALT

Monkfish cooks perfectly directly on top of the Aga 'a la plancha'. My preference is to do as little as possible with fish, often just a sprinkling of a few herbs and some salt is enough. You can make this brilliant all-purpose seasoning in a small spice grinder or a pestle and mortar and it will keep for weeks in a jar. Simply pick the rosemary leaves from 2 sprigs of rosemary about 100mm long, add them to 2 tablespoons of salt and a teaspoon of green peppercorns. Crush or blitz until you have a fine salt which will be, by now, greenish in colour. Sprinkle a little of the salt over 2 monkfish fillets, weighing about 200g each. Put a piece of Bake-O-Glide over the top of the simmering plate, rub the fish with a little olive oil and cook for 3-5 minutes per side until golden but still moist. Serve with olive oil and a couple of ripe tomatoes cut in half and lightly squeezed on the plate so that the juices amalgamate. Keep the Green Peppercorn Salt in an old jar for use with this and other fish dishes.

MONKFISH TAIL ROASTED WITH 50 CLOVES OF GARLIC

Garlic, when cooked this way, loses much of its pungency while its flavour becomes gloriously sweet. Much of the pleasure in this dish is to be had from squeezing the sweet cloves of garlic and enjoying them with the fish.

1 fennel bulb, very finely sliced
1 monkfish tail weighing about 1kg, skinned and
   membrane removed
50 cloves of garlic
4 tomatoes, cut in half
1 tbsp coriander seeds, lightly roasted and
   crushed
200-300ml extra virgin olive oil
A small handful of basil, finely chopped

Take a roasting dish and put the sliced fennel in a row down the middle. Sit the monkfish on top and put the cloves of garlic around the fish. Give the tomatoes a squeeze to release their juices and then add them to the dish. Sprinkle in the ground coriander and pour in the olive oil. Season. Roast on a grid shelf on the floor of the roasting oven for 40 minutes.

Remove the roasting dish and stir in the herbs. Either serve whole in the middle of the table or remove from the bone and serve with a spoonful of the vegetables and a good glug of oil.

Serves 4

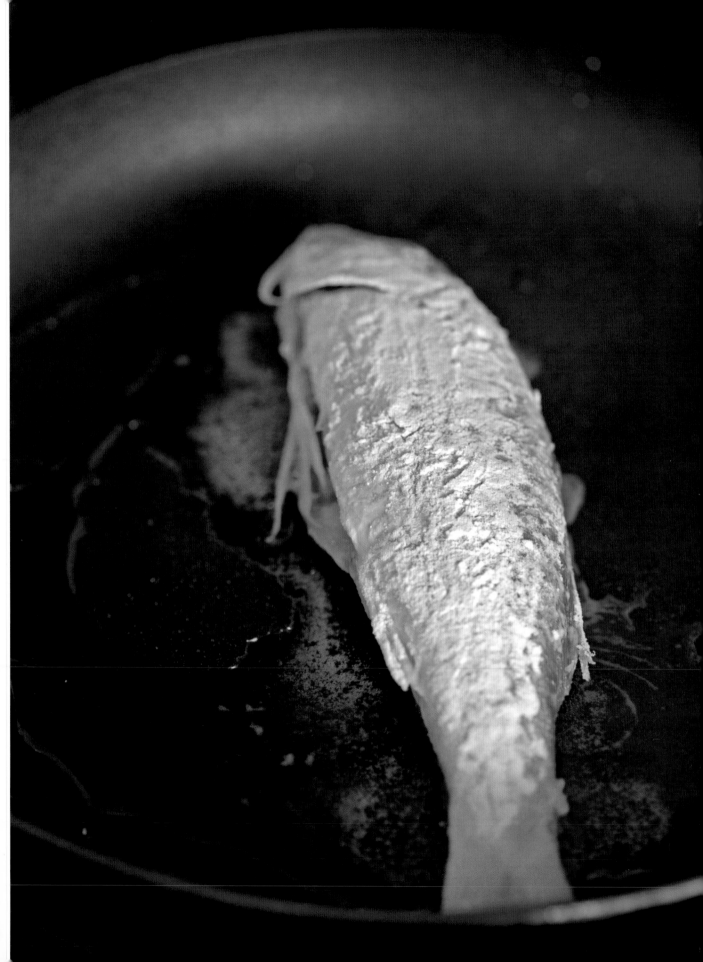

'RED MULLET IS MY FAVOURITE FISH – IT HAS A WONDERFUL FIRM TEXTURE, DELICIOUS SKIN AND FLESH THAT IS ALMOST SHELLFISH-LIKE.'

MUSSELS WITH INDIAN SPICES

This is a lovely, simple dish – but be warned, the spice mix is really quite fiery.

1-2kg mussels
1 tsp fenugreek
Seeds from 12 pods of cardamom
5 cloves
25cm of cinnamon stick
1 tsp black peppercorns
10 cloves of garlic
25cm piece of fresh ginger
A little oil for frying
1 tsp tomato purée
4 tbsps white wine vinegar
1½ tbsp sugar
Handful of fresh coriander, finely chopped
Handful of fresh mint, finely chopped

Steam open the mussels in a large pan on the boiling plate. Allow them to cool and remove the half shell. Reserve the juices.

Roast the fenugreek in the roasting oven. Whizz in a blender the roasted fenugreek with the cardamom seeds, the cloves, the cinnamon stick, black pepper, garlic and ginger. Fry this mixture in a little oil to cook the spices, garlic and ginger, this will take about 5-7 minutes. Add the tomato purée and then the white wine vinegar and sugar and cook for a further 6-7 minutes. inish by adding the fresh coriander and fresh mint and spoon over the mussels.

Serves 4 as a starter

MUSSELS WITH GLOUCESTER OLD SPOT AND BROAD BEANS

This is a great dish to be eating around September or October time when mussels are nice and fat. Serve bubbling from the pan with plenty of bread.

1.5kg mussels
15g butter
2 rashers thickly cut Old Spot bacon or good
    fatty back bacon, cut into small chunks
1 clove garlic, finely chopped
150ml double cream
A good handful of parsley, finely chopped
$1/2$ tsp mustard
Splash of Lea and Perrins sauce
400g broad beans
Fresh black pepper

Put the mussels in a dry pan, pop the lid on and place them on the boiling plate and allow them to open, shaking the pan from time to time. When cooled, remove them from their shells and reserve the cooking juices.

In a round paella dish or other dish suitable for taking to the table, melt the butter and then add the bacon and the garlic and cook until golden on the simmering plate. Add 4-5 tablespoons of the mussel juice, then the mussels, broad beans, and then the cream and stir in well. Add the parsley, mustard and a splash of Lea and Perrins. Season with lots of black pepper.

Serves 2

BOILED OCTOPUS WITH ROCKET, OIL AND VINEGAR

This recipe was given to me by my friend, Max, who runs the Gato Nero restaurant on the island of Burrano on the Venetian lagoon. It is probably one of the finest restaurants I have ever eaten in. Both Max's mother and father cook and you'd think their restaurant kitchen is actually a domestic one as the atmosphere is so relaxed. You can taste the confidence in the food – everything from the kitchen pleases. This is a real hidden quality that some cooks have without even realising it. There is usually plenty of fresh octopus available in Britain now, though it just doesn't often reach the fishmongers due to lack of demand. However, as it is quite usual to freeze octopus in order to help tenderise it, I think it perfectly acceptable to buy and use already frozen octopus. Look for octopus that are no longer than about 150mm.

2-3 small octopus per person, defrosted
Sea salt
Rocket leaves
Olive oil
Red wine vinegar

Bring a pan of water to the boil and add some sea salt. Holding the octopus by the head, carefully dip the ends of the tentacles into the boiling water to make them curl up – the traditional way for presentation on the plate. Gently lower the whole octopus into the water to be cooked, spinning them with your hand clockwise, which will again make the tentacles curl upwards. Gently simmer on the simmering plate for 30 minutes.

When cooked, remove them from the water and place them into a deep cereal bowl. Pour over a few ladlefuls of the cooking liquid and serve in the middle of the table.

Give your guests a plate of rocket, lightly dressed in olive oil and sea salt. Leave the oil and sea salt on the table with a bottle of red wine vinegar. Eat the octopus by spooning them whole from the liquid, sprinkling with salt and adding olive oil and vinegar to taste. I can promise you, they are absolutely delicious.

BEEF TARTARE WITH RAW OYSTERS

There is absolutely no cooking involved in this recipe, but I make the assumption that if you have taken the trouble to invest in an Aga then you really must love your food. I almost never put fish and meat together but this has got to be the one exception.

250g best beef fillet
1 egg yolk
A few tbsp of olive oil
1 tsp of French mustard
2 tbsp of capers, finely chopped
2 tbsp gherkins, finely chopped
Pinch of celery salt
8/9 crushed green peppercorns
A few dashes of Worcestershire sauce
A dash or two of Tabasco – to your taste
1 tbsp parsley, finely chopped
1 tbsp coriander, chopped
$\frac{1}{2}$ dozen shucked oysters
Black pepper

Finely chop the beef fillet with your favourite sharp knife.

In a bowl, whisk the egg yolk with the olive oil and mustard. Add the capers, gherkins, celery salt, peppercorns, Tabasco and Worcestershire sauce and whisk together. Add the finely chopped beef fillet and the herbs and mix well. Chop 5 of the oysters and stir into the beef mixture.

Simply serve on a pile on the plate, or if you wish, shape in a pastry ring, make a well on the top and sit a beautiful plump oyster in the middle. Season with a few turns of black pepper before tucking in. A nice addition is to add a few finely chopped anchovies, but these aren't essential as you already have the saltiness and freshness of the oysters.

Serves 2

POACHED OYSTERS WITH CHINESE SPICES

I prefer to eat my oysters straight from the shell and completely unadorned. I enjoy that wonderful sensation you get akin to putting your face in a rock pool. However, when oysters fatten up and become milky I have to admit to not being as fond of them. Their plumpness though makes them perfect for cooking, either roasted with a rich Rockafeller style butter (that is just butter whisked up with celery, chervil, parsley, spinach, Worcestershire sauce and breadcrumbs) or with a simple garlic butter. This more exotic oriental inspired alternative is fantastic and really easy to make.

25mm piece of ginger, peeled and cut into very fine slices
1 garlic clove, cut into very fine slices
50ml Chinese rice wine
100ml teriyaki marinade
Few splashes of light soy sauce
1 tbsp caster sugar
A few drops of sesame oil
25mm stick of cinnamon
1 star anise
6 rock oysters (don't even think about doing it with natives!)
3 spring onions, finely chopped
A handful of chopped coriander

Into a pan, put a cupful of water and all the ingredients apart from the oysters, spring onions and coriander. Place on the simmering plate and bring gently to a simmer for 4-5 minutes to allow the flavours to infuse. Taste and adjust the flavours by adding more soy or teriyaki If required – it should taste slightly fragrant and oriental.

Shuck the oysters and add them with their juices to the cooked broth. Add the chopped spring onions and continue to simmer for 2-3 minutes until the oysters are firm. Add the chopped coriander and spoon into bowls and serve.

Serves 2

POLLACK WITH YOUNG GREENS, ENGLISH MUSTARD AND SAGE

Pollack is a very underrated fish, but when really fresh can be excellent. Part of the reason that it gets such a bad press is probably down to its ugly name – I am tempted to start a campaign to change it to ensure future popularity! Because of its appearance, texture and taste, a name like 'golden cod' might suit it more....

Olive oil
2 pollack fillets, preferably cut from the top end of the fillet, weighing about 200g each
1 small young spring cabbage – spinach or broccoli leaves would also be fine
1 tsp English mustard
25g butter
1 tbsp capers
Small handful of parsley, chopped
Small handful of sage, finely chopped
A tiny splash of white wine vinegar
A squeeze of lemon
Black pepper

Heat some olive oil in a pan, suitable for the oven, on the boiling plate. Season the fish and place in the pan, flesh side down. Cook for 3-4 minutes until golden, then turn the fish and place the whole pan on the floor of the roasting oven. Cook for a further 2-3 minutes.

Steam the greens until wilted.

In a small pan, melt the butter, whisk in the mustard until properly emulsified and add the remaining ingredients. Toss the greens in the sauce to coat and season with plenty of black pepper. Serve the greens alongside the fish and spoon over any remaining sauce.

Serves 2

SPAGHETTI WITH PRAWNS AND TOMATO SAUCE

This is one of the simplest and most flavoursome pasta dishes I have ever cooked. Firstly you need some good home-made tomato sauce (see page 16) – don't attempt to make this with passata or tinned tomatoes, it just won't be the same. The process at the beginning of cooking, frying the sliced garlic and prawn heads in the oil, gives the dish real depth. To get the very best out of any prawn dish, choose your prawns carefully; try to buy only wild caught prawns – you will mainly see tiger prawns but do keep an eye out for pink and red shrimps (as they are commonly known) which are caught off the Spanish and Argentinian coast. I find these to be sweeter and, even when frozen, their flavour is everything you'd expect from shellfish of this sort. This is ideal recipe to serve in one dish for 2 to share – if you wish to serve 4, then simply double the ingredients. Remove the heads from 10 medium raw prawns (ask your fishmonger for 16/20 size to the kilo) and set aside. Peel the tails, throw away the shells, but keep the flesh and cut the prawn in half lengthways. Add a generous amount of oil to a paella or gratin dish and heat on the simmering plate of the Aga. Add 4 sliced garlic cloves, a pinch of salt and the reserved prawn heads.

Continue to fry until the garlic is golden and the heads turn colour – give them a squeeze with the back of the spoon to release any juices and meat in the head into the oil. Then remove the heads and garlic but keep the magnificent oil. Add the prawns to the oil and fry for 2-3 minutes. Add about 200-300ml (a small kilner jar) of tomato sauce and a handful of parsley. Heat through, season, and then add enough cooked spaghetti for 2. Toss with a pair of tongs, ensuring the pasta is thoroughly coated and serve.

ROCK SALMON BRAISED WITH CIDER, ROMAINE LETTUCE AND PEAS

I am a big fan of rock salmon, which is also known as flake, huss or dog fish. Its flesh is soft and white with a very delicate flavour. The braising liquid of cider with romaine lettuce and peas gives the dish a delicious sweetness.

20g butter
1 onion, finely chopped
350ml dry cider
1 piece of rock salmon, weighing about 500g, cut into 4 chunks
A handful of shredded romaine lettuce
A handful of fresh or frozen peas
A small handful of parsley, chopped

Place a paella pan or casserole on the simmering plate. Melt the butter and gently fry the onions until softened. Add the cider, boil to reduce by half and then add the pieces of fish and the lettuce. Cover and cook on a grid shelf on the floor of the roasting oven for 7-8 minutes.
Add the peas and the parsley and cook for a further 3-4 minutes. Season to taste and serve.

Serves 2

SEARED SCALLOPS WITH ROASTED GREEN PEPPER AND TOMATO SALAD

The salad that accompanies these seared scallops is extremely versatile. It is fabulously fresh with just a hint of spice and would go well with cod, plaice, turbot, brill, grey mullet and mackerel.

1 green pepper
4 ripe tomatoes, with the skins and seeds
   removed
A good pinch of cumin
A small handful of coriander
A small handful of parsley
1 clove of garlic, crushed to a paste with a little
   salt
Olive oil
6 large scallops
Sea salt and black pepper
lemon juice, to serve

Put the pepper in the roasting oven for 10-15 minutes until blackened. Remove and place in a plastic bag and seal it. Leave the pepper until it collapses and is soft and cooked through. Remove the skin and seeds and roughly chop the flesh.

Chop the tomato flesh in pieces the same size as the pepper and mix with the cumin, coriander, parsley, garlic, a little salt and a tablespoon or two of olive oil. Leave to one side to allow the flavours to develop for about 30 minutes.

Brush the scallops with oil and season with salt and black pepper. Place a ribbed grill pan on the boiling plate and cook the scallops for about 2-3 minutes on either side until golden and caramelised.

To serve, place a spoonful of the salad in the middle of each plate, place the scallops around and drizzle over some good olive oil, if needed, and a few drops of lemon juice.

Serves 2

SEARED SCALLOPS WITH BUTTERED WINTER CABBAGE, CHAMP AND PARSLEY SAUCE

Parsley sauce is delicious with any fish and is usually reserved for cod or haddock. Sadly it is often played around with by restaurants adding all sorts of flavours to it. It is absolutely delicious though made in the traditional way and paired with luxurious and sweet scallops and creamy champ (that's spring onion mash to you and me), loads of black pepper and buttered cabbage.

Half an onion
2 bay leaves
6 cloves
Few peppercorns
50g soft butter
2 tbsp flour
450ml milk
Handful of parsley leaf, finely chopped
500g potatoes, mashed
200ml double cream
6 spring onions, finely chopped
Sea salt and black pepper to season
8 scallops
1 small cabbage, finely chopped and blanched

Add the onion, bay leaf, cloves and peppercorns to the milk. (You can, if you wish, cut the onion, insert the bay leaves and then stick in the cloves thus making it easier to remove later.) Bring to the boil and leave to infuse for 15 minutes. Strain and set aside, discarding the onion and aromatics.

Melt 25g of the butter in the pan and sprinkle in the flour until you have a smooth paste – it should be of double cream consistency. Gradually pour on the milk until you have a sauce that coats the back of a spoon. Add the parsley and season to taste.

Warm the cream with the spring onions and then whisk into the mashed potato with the rest of the butter until luxuriously creamy. Season with salt and pepper. Set aside to keep warm in the simmering oven.

To cook the scallops, brush lightly with oil and season with salt and pepper. Put a piece of Bake-O-Glide on the simmering plate and cook them for 2 minutes or so on each side until caramelised and golden. Transfer to serving plates. Finally, add a little butter to a pan on the simmering plate, toss in the cabbage and swirl aroung and serve along with the champ, coating the dish with the parsley sauce.

Serves 2

SHRIMPS ON TOAST

You can easily buy packs of peeled crevettes gris or brown shrimps at most fishmongers these days. They are quite delicious. If you can find unpeeled, and have the time, then best of all is to peel them yourself. Make a small amount of béchamel sauce and when doing so add a splash of brandy to the roux before adding the milk. Throw in some parsley, some grated mace or nutmeg and a handful or so of peeled shrimps. Serve this mixture on thick buttered toast.

And, if you like, you could finish this off by sprinkling with a little Parmesan and cooking right at the top and the back of the roasting oven for a minute or two until the cheese is bubbling and golden.

ROASTED SKATE CHEEKS WITH ANCHOVY AND SHALLOT BUTTER

Skate cheeks are fabulous. They are wonderful nuggets of tender meat found in the body of the ray which joins to the wing. Most fishermen don't bother cutting them out because they have no perceived commercial value – so keep asking for them! That way we might create a demand and we might see more of them. When you do see them, ignore everything else on the counter and buy them like there's no tomorrow.

2 shallots, finely chopped
100ml red wine vinegar
6 salted anchovy fillets, finely chopped
A small handful of tarragon
Olive oil
Butter
400-500g skate cheeks, depending on appetite
Sea salt and black pepper

First make the butter by putting the shallots, red wine vinegar and anchovies in a pan on the simmering plate. Boil until the vinegar has reduced by two thirds and the anchovies have melted. Allow to cool and stir this mixture in with the softened butter and the tarragon.

Place an oval roasting dish on the simmering plate, add a little olive oil and a little butter. Season the skate cheeks with salt and pepper. Add the skate to the pan and cook for 4-5 minutes, turning occasionally until they are golden. Dot some of the anchovy and shallot butter around the bottom of the dish, place on the floor of the roasting oven and allow to cook for 5-6 minutes. Before serving, make sure the cheeks are well bathed in the butter. Boiled cabbage with plenty of black pepper is perfect with this.

Serves 2

FRIED SKATE FINGERS WITH CAPER SALAD

Fingers of skate aren't some wacky part of the fish that no one has yet discovered or doesn't want to eat, but rather big chunks of meat cut about 25mm from the middle of the wing, following the lines of the flesh. By preparing it this way, you get the lovely thick, sweet flesh with the soft bone in the middle (which is edible if you want to try it). Look for skate which is a nice bright pink and not a dull grey and has absolutely no smell of ammonia. If you've ever been told that skate needs to be left a few days, then cast aside this bit of advice, as it does nothing but bring on the vile smell and taste of ammonia.

4-5 tbsp good olive oil
1 tsp tarragon mustard
1 skate wing, weighing about 500g, cut into
   25mm fingers
Sea salt and black pepper
1 egg, beaten
A handful of fine, fresh breadcrumbs

For the Caper Salad
$1/2$ tsp tarragon mustard
2 tbsp red wine vinegar
125ml olive oil
2 tbsp salted capers, rinsed
A good handful of fresh flat leaf parsley
Zest of 1 lemon
1 shallot, finely chopped

Mix a little of the olive oil with half the mustard and brush over the skate wings. Season with a little salt and pepper. Dip the wings in the beaten egg, then the breadcrumbs, until you have a good coating. Heat some olive oil in a heavy bottomed roasting dish on the boiling plate, and fry the skate fingers on one side until crisp and golden. Turn them and then place the roasting tray directly on the floor of the roasting oven for a further 4-5 minutes until crisp and cooked through.

To make the caper salad, add half a teaspoon of tarragon mustard to the red wine vinegar, mixing together thoroughly. Then whisk in the olive oil to make a smooth emulsion. Mix the capers, parsley, lemon zest and shallot together. Mix with the dressing and serve alongside the skate. A spoonful of fresh mayonnaise also makes a nice accompaniment.

Serves 2

PAN-FRIED SKATE WITH CAPERS AND BLACK BUTTER

This is a classic way of cooking skate. I love black butter, so I never confine it just to skate. It works well with sole and especially plaice. I like to use really thick skate wings for this recipe and cut them into fingers and serve them as triangles on the plate, rather than the traditional slab of skate wing.

Olive oil for frying
2 thick skate wings, cut into fingers
40g unsalted butter
A glug of red wine vinegar
1 tbsp of capers
fresh parsley
1 lemon

Place a frying or oval pan on the boiling plate, add a little oil and allow to get hot. Add the skate fingers and cook for 3-4 minutes either side until golden. Remove from the pan and set aside and keep warm.

Add the butter to the hot pan and allow to melt until you have fine bubbles. Wait until the butter turns a deep brown and smells wonderfully nutty. Remove from the heat. Add a really good glug of red wine vinegar and stir to amalgamate with the butter. Add the capers and parsley. Transfer the fish to plates and spoon over the butter.
Serve with new potatoes and lemon wedges.

Serves 2

LEMON SOLE BAKED WITH BUTTER, LEMON AND PARSLEY

This is a nice way to serve a fish on the table for 2. A fish weighing about 600g is usually sufficient. As well as lemon sole this method would also work well with plaice, small dabs and pretty much any other flat fish. Take an oval roasting dish, suitable for taking to the table, rub the bottom with softened butter, lay the fish on top and then spread butter over the top of the fish. Place on a grid shelf in the middle of the roasting oven and cook for 6-7 minutes. Pull the fish out of the oven, tilt the dish and with a spoon baste the back of the fish with the melted butter. Replace and cook for a further 2-3 minutes, then repeat the basting process. The fish will be cooked after about 15 minutes and the fins will be crisp and golden. On removal from the oven and just before serving, tilt the dish, add some parsley and the juice of about 1/2 a lemon to the buttery juices, and then finally baste the fish again, making sure you have a good covering of the parsley and juices. If at any time during cooking you feel there isn't enough butter in the pan, just add more.

CHILLI SALT AND PEPPER SQUID

The flavours in this squid dish appeal to everyone, and when served with some cold beer makes for a great supper. The secret here is to make sure that the oil is really hot so that you get a lovely crisp coating on the squid. This also works well in the Aga wok, stir-fried in hot oil – just leave out the flour and add the rest of the ingredients as you stir-fry.

A handful of flour
1 tbsp of salt
1 tbsp of ground white peppercorns
1 tsp of finely ground Szechuan peppercorns
1 tsp finely ground black peppercorns
1 tbsp of hot chilli powder
400g whole squid, cleaned
Olive oil
A handful of chopped coriander
Lemon for squeezing

Combine the flour, salt, peppercorns and chilli powder and toss the squid in it. Take a heavy roasting pan or small paella dish and add some olive oil. Get it really hot on the boiling plate, add the squid and fry until crisp on one side. Turn the squid and place the pan on the floor of the roasting oven and continue to cook for a further 4-5 minutes. Remove from the oven, drain off any juices and sprinkle with coriander and lemon juice.

Serves 2

'TUNA SHOULD BE SEARED ON THE OUTSIDE, VERY PINK IN THE MIDDLE, BUT NOT COLD, AND THE HEAT SHOULD PENETRATE THROUGH THE STEAK JUST ENOUGH TO LOOSEN THE MEMBRANE BETWEEN THE FLAKES.'

MIXED SEAFOOD

'WHEN IT COMES TO BUYING SHELLFISH, DON'T BE PRECISE, BUY A MIXTURE OF WHAT IS THERE AND WHAT YOU FANCY.'

SPAGHETTI WITH SEAFOOD, FRESH TOMATO, OLIVE OIL AND PARSLEY

This is a great dish. It makes the best of a bit of everything that you might expect to find at your fishmongers. Be flexible, any fish or shellfish is fine (except mackerel and other oily fish such as tuna and perhaps salmon). Instead of using fresh tomatoes you could just add, as an alternative, some Fresh Tomato Sauce (see page 16).

Small glass dry white wine
200g mussels in their shells
200g clams in their shells
75ml good olive oil
1 clove of garlic, chopped
6 raw prawns, peeled
6 langoustines, blanched and then peeled
100g monkfish fillet, sliced
2 scallops, sliced
3 tomatoes, skinned
Small handful of parsley
Pinch of sea salt
Enough cooked spaghetti for two (let your appetite dictate, but I reckon on 75g per person)

Put the wine in a pan on the hot plate and bring to the boil, add the mussels and clams and cover. When they have all opened remove from the heat (discard any that have not opened) and leave to cool slightly. When cool enough to handle remove the meat from the shells and reserve the cooking liquid.

In a large frying, roasting or Aga paella pan, heat the olive oil on the simmering plate and add the garlic and allow to colour. Add the peeled raw prawns, langoustines, scallops and monkfish and fry gently for 3-4 minutes. Add the meat from the clams and mussels, and then squeeze in the tomatoes so that some of the juice mixes into the oil. Add the parsley, a few tablespoons of the reserved cooking liquid and simmer for 2-3 minutes. Add the spaghetti to the pan and toss it around to warm through quickly and serve.

Serves 2

ZUPPA DA PESCATORE

This is a brilliant recipe from my first book, *FishWorks Seafood Café Cookbook*, which has fast become a firm favourite in our Fishworks restaurants. Any selection of fish and shellfish can be used for this fantastic Portuguese fish soup – lobster, clams, mussels, chunks of skate, steaks of hake, gurnard and cod, the choice is yours. But be sure to buy enough to fill the pan packed tightly in one layer.

1 shallot, finely chopped
2 cloves of garlic, chopped
Olive oil
2 roasted tomatoes
Pinch of saffron
3 or 4 sprigs of thyme
Splash Pernod or anise
A selection of fish (see introduction above)
575ml fish stock
Sea salt
Fresh chopped parsley or basil for sprinkling
    over the top – or both
Grilled bread, to serve (optional)
Aioli, to serve (optional)

In a large pan on the simmering plate, sweat the shallots and garlic in the olive oil. Add the tomatoes, saffron and thyme and stir together. Add the Pernod and boil to reduce by two thirds, allowing the alcohol to evaporate.

Add the fish and cover with fish stock. Simmer for 8-10 minutes. Remove the thyme and season. Finally, sprinkle with fresh chopped herbs and, if you like, some grilled bread topped with rich garlicky aioli).

Serves 4

DISHES TO SHARE

A CRAB SUPPER

Some fish are just better served whole or on the bone, in the middle of the table for guests to dig in. There is nothing better than serving half a turbot, a chunk or salmon or a pile of crabs straight from the cooker for all to share. This small section of four of my favourite dishes to share are tried and tested, delicious and, above all, simple.

A crab supper makes for a perfect start to the weekend – an informal meal with the family of simply boiled crab, mayonnaise, bread and wine. I am lucky that my dining table is an old fishmonger's slab, so it is well used to the battering and abuse that comes with smashing open whole crabs – you may decide to do your smashing and grabbing outside on an old table, or just cover your kitchen table inside with a board to protect it. Once you have decided on a suitable surface, cover it with plenty of newspaper to contain all the debris. Now you are ready to get going – put two or three crabs, a big bowl of freshly made mayonnaise, some chilled wine, a couple of small hammers, some picks and some nut crackers on the table and get stuck in.

A quick note on cooking crabs
If possible it is always best to cook crabs yourself. Get a big pan, fill it with water and put in a handful of salt. Bring to the boil, and add the crab and cook for 15-18 minutes. Drain and stand the crab on its nose to cool.

A quick note on dealing with crabs
Nothing in a crab is harmful. Open them up by first turning them upside down on their shells with their back facing you. Then put your hands around the sides of them and use your thumbs to break the body away from the top shell.
This can be quite difficult to do but a bit of brute force usually does the trick. You will see the 'dead men's fingers' sticking up at the edge of the body – give them a tug and discard them. Everything else, from the brown meat in the shell, to the wonderful sweet meat hidden in the honeycomb of pockets inside the body that the legs are attached to, is edible and quite deliciously sweet.

'A CRAB SUPPER MAKES FOR A PERFECT START TO THE WEEKEND.'

MONKFISH JOINT ROASTED WITH POTATOES, ROSEMARY AND GARLIC

This is a brilliant dish. Monkfish, which I personally think is overrated, has a fine texture but does lack just a little in the flavour stakes. However, made up into a joint, seared until crisp, roasted and served in its own juices, with these fabulous roast potatoes, makes for a fine Sunday lunch. If you like to eat a sauce with your fish then I suggest a simple hollandaise or béarnaise – a bowl of fried spinach with garlic would also be good.

1 monkfish tail, weighing about 1.2-1.4kg
   (ask your fishmonger to skin it, fillet it and
   remove the membranes from the fillets)
4 salted anchovies
2 garlic cloves, finely sliced
A few sprigs of rosemary
Some butcher's string
Salt and pepper

For the potatoes
Enough potatoes for 4, peeled and cut into
   20mm cubes
A few sprigs of rosemary
Some flour
Sea salt
About 15 whole cloves of garlic, roasted in
   their skins with salt and olive oil for about
   10 minutes in the roasting oven
Parsley, to serve
Lemon juice, to serve

Lay the fish fillets out on a board. You will notice that each fillet has a flat side, which is where the bone would have been. Lay one of the fillets with this side facing uppermost and lay the four anchovy fillets crossways down the fish. Slice the garlic and then lay on as well, then the rosemary. Take the other fillet with the flat side facing down and place the thick end against the thin end of the fillet which is on the board. If you roll this onto its side you should now have a cylindrical joint with your herbs and anchovies sandwiched between the two. Take some butcher's string and tie it round the joint in 25mm spaces, nice and tight.

Add some olive oil to a frying pan on the boiling plate, season the monkfish with a little salt and pepper and sear all over until golden. Set aside, ready for the oven.

Blanch the potatoes until just softened. Drain through a colander and allow to steam dry. Sieve over some flour and toss in the colander to make sure they are well coated. Take the roasting tin in which the garlic cloves were roasted, add a little more olive oil and place on the floor of the roasting oven to get the oil really hot. Tip in the potatoes with the garlic, stir thoroughly to ensure they are well coated with the olive oil. Add the sprigs of rosemary and place on the floor of the roasting oven for about 10-15 minutes.

Remove the potatoes from the oven and add the seared monkfish, put back in the oven and cook for a further 10-15 minutes until the fish is just cooked and the potatoes are crisp and golden. If the potatoes cook before the fish, simply remove them and keep hot, and continue cooking the fish.

To serve, cut the monkfish into equal chunks, stand them on their ends, sprinkle with parsley and a few drops of lemon juice. Season the whole tray with sea salt and serve.

Serves 4

BAKED SALMON OR COD WITH PROSECCO AND FRESH HERBS

Salmon and cod are two of my favourite fish for cooking this way, though this method would work with just about any fish. It is really colourful and vibrant and makes a great centrepiece. Serve with mashed potato or a simple garden salad. Prosecco is the favoured drink of Venetians. A light sparkling fresh clean taste is what you can expect from this wine. It is one of those wines that you can drink all day long and is perfect for cooking fish in.

$^1/_2$ a bottle of Prosecco
A wine glass of water
6-8 ripe tomatoes, cut in half
A good sized bunch of basil
A few sprigs of fresh thyme
Some whole garlic cloves
A few sprigs of rosemary
1 tbsp of Worcestershire sauce
1 chunk of salmon, cut from the middle of the fish (I think this is the best part), weighing about 800g (or 1 piece of cod fillet from the thick end of the fish weighing about 600-800g)
Salt and black pepper

Simply put all the ingredients except for the fish in a pan with a tight fitting lid and place on the boiling plate, giving the tomatoes a squeeze as you do so to bring out their juices. Bring to the boil. Place the fish on top, cover and place on a shelf in the middle of the roasting oven for between 15–20 minutes. Taste the juices, season with salt and pepper and serve.

When serving salmon, I like to peel the skin off (it comes off easily) to show off the flesh.

Serves 4

'COD COOKED IN PROSECCO WITH FRESH HERBS IS ONE OF MY FAVOURITE DISHES – COLOURFUL AND VIBRANT, IT IS A GREAT CENTREPIECE FOR THE TABLE.'

BRAISED TURBOT WITH CARAMELISED FENNEL, OLIVES AND BASIL

You can use a whole turbot for this dish but unfortunately a fish weighing over about 2kg won't fit comfortably into the Aga's oven, and I think with turbot, the bigger the fish the better the experience. So this is a chance for you to be able to really take advantage of your fishmonger. Ask him for a fish which weighs in excess of 4kg. Tell him you want it cut down the backbone, from the head to tail and you want the left hand side – this is the thickest and best meat of the fish. The other side, while still excellent to eat has the belly cavity which you can do little with. I would recommend allowing about 300-350g of turbot on the bone per person, so a 1kg piece would serve 3 or just about 4 if it were a light lunch.

Olive oil
2 fennel bulbs, trimmed and sliced – it doesn't
   really matter which way you slice it
1 tsp fennel seeds, lighlty crushed
1 onion, sliced
2 garlic cloves, finely sliced
Splash of Pernod
1 large glass of dry white wine
A handful of basil, finely chopped
700g piece of turbot
Salt
A handful of good quality black olives with
   stones squeezed out
Juice of 1/2 a lemon

Add some olive oil to a large pan on the simmering plate. Add the fennel and lightly crushed fennel seeds and onion. Cook gently for 4-5 minutes until the onion starts to soften, then add the garlic and cook for another minute or two. Add the Pernod and allow this to evaporate almost completely, then add the wine and boil for a minute or two to burn off the alcohol.

Add half of the basil and transfer to an oval roasting dish, big enough to hold the fish. Lay the fish on top, season with salt and place in the top of the roasting oven for 15 minutes. Remove, sprinkle the olives around the fish and return to the oven for a further 5 minutes. When cooked the fish should exude a white milky liquid. Remove from the oven. Carefully peel the skin from the turbot – it should come away easily but may be just a bit hot, so a cloth often helps. Spoon some of the cooking juices over the fish, squeeze half the lemon over the top, sprinkle with the remaining basil, a little sea salt and serve.

Serves 2

INDEX

ACKNOWLEDGEMENTS

This book wouldn't have been possible without the help and support of the following – I owe them all big thanks:

Roy Morris for his fabulous support, friendship and enthusiasm – you're brilliant. Mat (The Clam) Prowse, a truly great chef and friend – big thanks always. To Louise Bunce, Simon Page and Richard Maggs at Aga. My wonderful agent Dinah Wiener. To Jon Croft, Matt Inwood and Meg Avent at Absolute Press, with whom it's always a pleasure to work – thanks for your great patience and enthusiasm for this project right from the start. Jason Lowe for his brilliant photography, laughter (and food styling!). To Isobel, who is a daily joy, this book is for you. Sadie, hope this book gets you to try just a little fish! Ben Tonks, Fran and Blue – big thanks always for getting involved. My best mate Ad. Laura Cowan, my great assistant and friend, for organising my life so that I am able to do this – big, big thanks. Many thanks to all the great people at FishWorks past and present without whom none of this would be possible. And lastly, my biggest thanks, for just about everything, to the most lovely person I know, Pen, x.